What Will the Weather Be Like Today?

Also illustrated by Kazuko
Cuckoobush Farm

Also by Paul Rogers
From Me to You

What Will the Weather Be Like Today?

PAUL ROGERS

PICTURES BY KAZUKO

SILVER BURDETT GINN

Needham, MA   Parsippany, NJ

Atlanta, GA   Deerfield, IL   Irving, TX   Santa Clara. CA

Pour la famille Bony
P.R.

To my mother
From Kazuko

SILVER BURDETT GINN

A Division of Simon & Schuster
160 Gould Street
Needham Heights, MA 02194–2310

Simon & Schuster edition, 1996

4 5 6 7 8 9 10 SP 01 00 99 98 97

ISBN : SSB 0–663–59142–2
BSB 0–663–59125–2

Just at the moment
when night becomes day,
when the stars in the sky
begin fading away,

you can hear all the birds
and the animals say,

"What will the weather be like today?"

Will it be windy?

9

Will it be warm?

Will there be snow?

Or a frost?

Or a storm?

"Be dry," says the lizard,
"and *I* won't complain."

The frog in the bog says,
"Perhaps it will rain."

The white cockatoo
likes it steamy and hot.

The mole doesn't know if it's raining or not.

"Whatever the weather,
I work," says the bee.

"Wet," says the duck,
"is the weather for me."

"Weather? What's that?"

say the fish in the sea.

The world has awakened.
The day has begun,

and somewhere it's cloudy,

and somewhere there's sun,

and somewhere the sun
and the rain meet to play,

and paint a bright rainbow to dress up the day!

How is the weather where *you* are today?